on
FAITH

Other Pope Francis books by Loyola Press

on FAITH

POPE FRANCIS

LOYOLA PRESS.
A JESUIT MINISTRY
Chicago

LOYOLA PRESS.
A JESUIT MINISTRY

3441 N. Ashland Avenue
Chicago, Illinois 60657
(800) 621-1008
www.loyolapress.com

Cover art credit: iStock.com/ROMAOSLO.

ISBN: 978-0-8294-4862-7
Library of Congress Control Number: 2018959649

Printed in the United States of America.
18 19 20 21 22 23 24 25 26 27 TShore 10 9 8 7 6 5 4 3 2 1

Man is faithful when he believes in God and his promises;
God is faithful when he grants to man what he has promised.
—SAINT AUGUSTINE

Contents

Contents

Contents

Editor's Note

Pope Francis tells us that faith is a journey—for Christians, a journey that begins in Bethlehem with birth and ends in Jerusalem with death on a cross, which turns out not to be the end at all. That's just the outline of our faith story, the microcosm of a mystery vast and transformative. Jesus, the person born to Mary, through his journey of faith becomes the Christ and, in so doing, alters time, history, salvation, and death itself.

It is no easy task to follow Christ in faith, but Pope Francis encourages us: "This is the real journey: to walk with the Lord always, even at moments of weakness, even in our sins. Never to prefer a makeshift path of our own. . . . Faith is ultimate fidelity, like that of Mary."

We cannot know in advance what we will encounter on this journey because the path is revealed only in the walking: "Our life is not given to us like an opera libretto, in which all is written down; but rather faith means going, walking, doing, searching, seeing. . . . We must enter into the adventure of the quest for meeting God; and we must let God search and encounter us."

For Pope Francis, faith is a movement, a path we follow each and every day: "Remember this always: faith is walking with Jesus; and it is a walk that lasts a lifetime. At the end there shall be the definitive encounter. Certainly, at some moments on the journey we feel tired and confused. But the faith gives us the certainty of Jesus' constant presence in every situation, even the most painful or difficult to understand. We are called to walk in order to enter ever more deeply into the mystery of the love of God, which reigns over us and permits us to live in serenity and hope."

Faith is also a gift received, a love placed deep in our hearts that seeks restlessly for the heart of Christ. Faith allows us to see with new eyes and to join in the epic sojourn of salvation upon which the Church has embarked: "Faith . . . enables us to become part of the Church's great pilgrimage through history until the end of the world. For those who have been transformed in this way, a new way of seeing opens up, faith becomes light for their eyes."

Into the formless void, our Creator God said, "Let there be light." And the sun shone brightly on the Lord's creation, where before there was nothing. Jesus, waiting upon the shores of the Sea of Galilee, with a small charcoal fire burning faintly in the darkness, guided the disciples safely to land after a long night of fishing. This is our God, a God great and small, who honors and keeps his faith with us.

Turning again to the words of Pope Francis: "Faith is not a light that scatters all our darkness but a lamp that guides our steps in the night and suffices for the journey."

I pray that faith will light your way as you move toward an encounter with the living God, who in the mystery of faith is both destination and companion.

Joseph Durepos
Chicago, June 2018

1
Confessing Jesus

Let us ask ourselves if we are *parlor Christians*, who love to chat about how things are going in the Church and the world, or if we are *apostles on the go*, who confess Jesus with our lives because we hold him in our hearts. We who confess Jesus know that we are not simply to offer opinions but to offer our very lives. We know that we are not to believe half-heartedly but to "be on fire" with love. We know that we cannot just "tread water" or take the easy way out but have to risk putting out into the deep, daily renewing our self-offering.

2
True Faith

True faith is that which makes us more charitable, more merciful, more honest, and more humane. It moves our hearts to love everyone without counting the cost, without distinction, and without preference. It makes us see the other not as an enemy to be overcome but as a brother or sister to be loved, served, and helped. It spurs us on to spread, defend, and live out the culture of encounter, dialogue, respect, and fraternity.

3

Growing in Faith

Faith gives us the courage to forgive those who have wronged us, to extend a hand to the fallen, to clothe the naked, to feed the hungry, to visit the imprisoned, to help orphans, to give drink to those who thirst, and to come to the aid of the elderly and those in need. True faith leads us to protect the rights of others with the same zeal and enthusiasm with which we defend our own rights. Indeed, the more we grow in faith and knowledge, the more we grow in humility and in the awareness of our littleness.

4
By Faith

Abraham left his home without knowing where he was going, by faith. All our ancestors in the faith died seeing the good that was promised, but from a distance. Our life is not given to us like an opera libretto, in which all is written down; rather, faith means going, walking, doing, searching, seeing. We must enter into the adventure of the quest for meeting God; and we must let God search and encounter us.

5

A Faith That Calls Us by Name

Something disturbing takes place in Abraham's life: God speaks to him; he reveals himself as a God who speaks and calls his name. Faith is linked to hearing. Abraham does not see God but hears his voice. Faith thus takes on a personal aspect. God is not the god of a particular place or a deity linked to specific sacred time, but the God of a person, the God of Abraham, Isaac, and Jacob, capable of interacting with us and establishing a covenant with us. Faith is our response to a word that engages us personally, to a "Thou" who calls us by name.

6

Faith Is a Call and a Promise

The word spoken to Abraham contains both a call and a promise. First, it is a call to leave his own land, a summons to a new life, the beginning of an exodus that points him toward an unforeseen future. The sight that faith would give Abraham would always be linked to the need to take this step forward: faith "sees" to the extent that it journeys, to the extent that it chooses to enter the horizons opened up by God's word.

7

Abraham's Faith

Abraham is asked to entrust himself to [God's] word. Faith understands that something so apparently ephemeral and fleeting as a word, when spoken by the God who is fidelity, becomes absolutely certain and unshakable, guaranteeing the continuity of our journey through history. Faith accepts this word as a solid rock upon which we can build, a straight highway on which we can travel.

For Abraham, faith in God sheds light on the depths of his being; it enables him to acknowledge the wellspring of goodness at the origin of all things and to realize that his life is not the product of nonbeing or chance but the fruit of a personal call and a personal love. The mysterious God who called him is no alien deity but the God who is the origin and mainstay of all that is. The great test of Abraham's faith—the sacrifice of his son Isaac—would show the extent to which this primordial love is capable of ensuring life, even beyond death.

8

Faith Teaches

God calls Abraham to go forth from his land and promises to make of him a great nation, a great people on whom the divine blessing rests. As salvation history progresses, it becomes evident that God wants to make everyone share as brothers and sisters in that one blessing, which attains its fullness in Jesus, so that all may be one.

The boundless love of our Father also comes to us, in Jesus, through our brothers and sisters. Faith teaches us to see that every man and woman represents a blessing for me, that the light of God's face shines on me through the faces of my brothers and sisters.

9

The Faith of Israel

In the faith of Israel we also encounter the figure of Moses, the mediator. The people may not see the face of God; it is Moses who speaks to YHWH on the mountain and then tells the others of the Lord's will. With this presence of a mediator in its midst, Israel learns to journey together in unity. The individual's act of faith finds its place within a community, within the common "we" of the people who, in faith, are like a single person—"my first-born son," as God would describe all of Israel (Ex. 4:22). Here mediation is not an obstacle but an opening; through our encounter with others, our gaze rises to a truth greater than ourselves.

10

Faith and the Decalogue

The link between faith and the Decalogue [the Ten Commandments] is important. Faith, as we have said, takes the form of a journey, a path to be followed, which begins with an encounter with the living God. It is in the light of faith, of complete entrustment to the God who saves, that the Ten Commandments take on their deepest truth, as seen in the words that introduce them: "I am the Lord your God, who brought you out of the land of Egypt" (Ex. 20:2).

The Decalogue is not a set of negative commands. Rather, it provides concrete directions for emerging from the desert of the selfish and self-enclosed ego to enter into dialogue with God, to be embraced by his mercy and then to bring that mercy to others. Faith thus professes the love of God—the origin and upholder of all things—and lets itself be guided by this love to journey toward the fullness of communion with God.

The Decalogue appears as the path of gratitude, the response of love, made possible because in faith we are receptive to the experience of God's transforming love for us. And this path receives new light from Jesus' teaching in the Sermon on the Mount (Matt. 5–7).

11

Biblical Faith

At the heart of biblical faith is God's love, his concrete concern for every person, and his plan of salvation, which embraces all of humanity and all of creation, culminating in the incarnation, death, and resurrection of Jesus Christ. Without insight into these realities, there is no criterion for discerning what makes human life precious and unique. Man loses his place in the universe; he is cast adrift in nature, either renouncing his proper moral responsibility or else presuming to be a sort of absolute judge, endowed with an unlimited power to manipulate the world around him.

12
The Light of Faith

Israel's confession of faith takes shape as an account of God's deeds in setting his people free and acting as their guide; this account is passed down from one generation to the next. God's light shines for Israel through the remembrance of the Lord's mighty deeds, recalled and celebrated in worship and passed down from parents to children. Here we see how the light of faith is linked to concrete life stories, to the grateful remembrance of God's mighty deeds and the progressive fulfillment of his promises.

13

Faith Perceives

The word that God speaks to us in Jesus is not simply one word among many but his eternal Word (Heb. 1:1–2). God can give no greater guarantee of his love, as Saint Paul reminds us (Rom. 8:31–39). Christian faith is thus faith in a perfect love, in its decisive power, in its ability to transform the world and to unfold its history. "We know and believe the love that God has for us" (1 John 4:16). In the love of God revealed in Jesus, faith perceives the foundation on which all reality and its final destiny rest.

14
Faith and Remembrance

Remembrance is essential for faith, as water is for a plant. A plant without water cannot stay alive and bear fruit. Nor can faith, unless it drinks deeply of the memory of all that the Lord has done for us. Remember Jesus Christ.

15
God's Gift of Faith

God's gift of faith is a supernaturally infused virtue, and we realize that a great love has been offered us, a good word has been spoken to us, and that when we welcome that word—Jesus Christ the Word made flesh—the Holy Spirit transforms us, lights up our way to the future, and enables us joyfully to advance along that way on wings of hope. Thus wonderfully interwoven, faith, hope, and charity become the driving force of the Christian life as it advances toward full communion with God.

16

Christian Faith

Christian faith is centered on Christ; it is the confession that Jesus is Lord and that God has raised him from the dead. All the threads of the Old Testament converge in Christ; he becomes the definitive "Yes" to all the promises, the ultimate basis of our "Amen" to God (2 Cor. 1:20).

The history of Jesus is the complete manifestation of God's reliability. If Israel continued to recall God's great acts of love, which formed the core of its confession of faith and broadened its gaze in faith, then the life of Jesus now appears as the locus of God's definitive intervention, the supreme manifestation of his love for us.

17

Our Faith

Christian faith is faith in the incarnation of the Word and his bodily resurrection; it is faith in a God who is so close to us that he entered our human history. Far from divorcing us from reality, our faith in the Son of God made man in Jesus of Nazareth enables us to grasp reality's deepest meaning and to see how much God loves this world and is constantly guiding it toward himself. This leads us, as Christians, to live our lives in this world with ever-greater commitment and intensity.

18
The Touch of Faith

Christ came down to earth and rose from the dead; by his incarnation and resurrection, the Son of God embraced the whole of human life and history and now dwells in our hearts through the Holy Spirit. Faith knows that God has drawn close to us, that Christ has been given to us as a great gift that inwardly transforms us, dwells within us, and thus bestows on us the light that illumines the origin and the end of life.

In faith, we can touch him and receive the power of his grace. Saint Augustine, commenting on the account of the woman suffering from hemorrhages who touched Jesus and was cured, says: "To touch him with our hearts: that is what it means to believe" (Luke 8:45–46). The crowd presses in on Jesus, but they do not reach him with the personal touch of faith, which apprehends the mystery that he is the Son who reveals the Father. Only when we are configured to Jesus do we receive the eyes needed to see him.

19

Faith Walking with Jesus

Our faith, the Church that Christ willed, is not based on an idea, it is not based on a philosophy; it is based on Christ himself. And the Church is like a plant that over the long centuries has grown, has developed, and has borne fruit. Yet her roots are planted firmly in him and that fundamental experience of Christ that the apostles had, chosen and sent out by Jesus, reaching all the way to us. From this little plant to our day, this is how the Church has spread everywhere in the world. Faith is walking with Jesus.

Remember this always: faith is walking with Jesus, and it is a walk that lasts a lifetime. At the end there shall be the definitive encounter. Certainly, at some moments on the journey, we feel tired and confused. But the faith gives us the certainty of Jesus' constant presence in every situation, even the most painful or difficult to understand. We are called to walk in order to enter ever more deeply into the mystery of the love of God, which reigns over us and permits us to live in serenity and hope.

20
Light of Faith

Faith, received from God as a supernatural gift, becomes a light for our way, guiding our journey through time. On the one hand, it is a light coming from the past, the light of the foundational memory of the life of Jesus that revealed his perfectly trustworthy love, a love capable of triumphing over death.

21

Faith, A Light for Our Darkness

The lamp is a symbol of the faith that illuminates our life, while the oil is a symbol of the charity that nourishes the light of faith, making it fruitful and credible. The condition for being prepared for the encounter with the Lord is not only faith but also a Christian life abundant with love and charity for our neighbor.

Yet because Christ has risen and draws us beyond death, faith is also a light coming from the future and opening before us vast horizons that guide us beyond our isolated selves toward the breadth of communion. We come to see that faith does not dwell in shadow and gloom; it is a light for our darkness.

22
Faith in Jesus

Christian faith in Jesus, the one Savior of the world, proclaims that all God's light is concentrated in him, in his "luminous life," which discloses the origin and the end of history. There is no human experience, no journey of man to God, that cannot be taken up, illumined, and purified by this light. The more Christians immerse themselves in the circle of Christ's light, the more capable they become of understanding and accompanying the path of every man and woman toward God.

Faith by its very nature demands renouncing the immediate possession that sight would appear to offer. It is an invitation to turn to the source of the light while respecting the mystery of a countenance that will unveil itself personally in its own good time.

23

Faith Is Passed On

The light of Christ shines, as in a mirror, upon the face of Christians. As it spreads, it comes down to us so that we too can share in that vision and reflect that light to others—in the same way that, in the Easter liturgy, the light of the paschal candle lights countless other candles. Faith is passed on, we might say, by contact, from one person to another, just as one candle is lit from another. Christians, in their poverty, plant a seed so rich that it becomes a great tree, capable of filling the world with its fruit.

24

The Lamp of Our Faith

If we allow ourselves to be guided by what seems more comfortable, by seeking our own interests, then our life becomes barren, incapable of giving life to others, and we accumulate no reserve of oil for the lamp of our faith; and this—faith—will be extinguished at the moment of the Lord's coming, or even before. If, instead, we are watchful and seek to do good, with acts of love, of sharing, and of service to a neighbor in difficulty, then we can be at peace while we wait for the bridegroom to come. The Lord can come at any moment, and even the slumber of death does not frighten us, because we have a reserve of oil, accumulated through everyday good works. Faith inspires charity, and charity safeguards faith.

25

Faith in Idols

In place of faith in God, it can sometimes seem better to worship an idol, into whose face we can look directly and whose origin we know because it is the work of our own hands. Before an idol, there is no risk that we will be called to abandon our security, for idols "have mouths, but they cannot speak" (Ps. 115:5).

Idols exist, we begin to see, as a pretext for setting ourselves at the center of reality and worshipping the work of our own hands. Once we have lost the fundamental orientation that unifies our existence, we break down into the multiplicity of our desires. When we refuse to await the time of promise, our life story disintegrates into a myriad of unconnected instants. Idolatry, then, is always polytheism, an aimless passing from one lord to another.

26

Faith, Tied to Conversion

Idolatry does not offer a journey but rather a plethora of paths leading nowhere and forming a vast labyrinth. Those who choose not to put their trust in God must hear the din of countless idols crying out: "Put your trust in me!"

Jesus' admonition is always pertinent; today, too, we form an idea of God that prevents us from enjoying God's real presence. Some people carve out a "do-it-yourself" faith that reduces God to the limited space of one's own desires and convictions. This faith is not a conversion to the Lord who reveals himself but, rather, it prevents us from enlivening our life and consciousness.

Faith, tied as it is to conversion, is the opposite of idolatry; it breaks with idols to turn to the living God in a personal encounter. Believing means entrusting oneself to a merciful love that always accepts and pardons, that sustains and directs our lives, and that shows its power by its ability to make straight the crooked lines of our history. Faith consists in the willingness to let ourselves be constantly transformed and renewed by God's call. . . . By constantly turning toward the Lord, we discover a sure path that liberates us from the dissolution imposed upon us by idols.

27

Faith, Turned in On Itself

Those who reduce God to a false idol use his holy name to justify their own interests, or actual hatred and violence. For others, God is only a psychological refuge in which to be reassured in difficult moments: this is a faith turned in on itself, impervious to the power of the merciful love of Jesus, which reaches out to others.

Others still consider Christ only as a good instructor of ethical teachings, one among the many [teachers in our] history. There are those who stifle the faith in a purely intimate relationship with Jesus, nullifying his missionary thrust that is capable of transforming the world and history. We Christians believe in the God of Jesus Christ, and our desire is that of growing in the living experience of his mystery of love.

28

Real Faith Is Communal

Faith is not a private matter, a completely individualistic notion, or a personal opinion: it comes from hearing, and it is meant to find expression in words and to be proclaimed. For "how are they to believe in him of whom they have never heard? And how are they to hear without a preacher?" (Rom. 10:14).

The Church, at the beginning of her life and of her mission in the world, was but a community constituted to confess faith in Jesus Christ the Son of God and Redeemer of [humanity], a faith that operates through love. They go together! In today's world, too, the Church is called to be the community in the world that, rooted in Christ through baptism, humbly and courageously professes faith in him, witnessing to it in love.

29

The Measure of Faith

The life of the believer . . . is a life lived in the Church. When Saint Paul tells the Christians of Rome that all who believe in Christ make up one body, he urges them not to boast of this; rather, each must think of himself "according to the measure of faith that God has assigned" (Rom. 12:3). Those who believe come to see themselves in the light of the faith they profess: Christ is the mirror in which they find their own image fully realized.

Just as Christ gathers to himself all those who believe and makes them his body, so the Christians come to see themselves as members of this body, in an essential relationship with all other believers. The image of a body does not imply that the believer is simply one part of an anonymous whole, a mere cog in a great machine; rather, [this image] brings out the vital union of Christ with believers and of believers among themselves.

30
The Profession of Faith

Apart from this body, outside this unity of the Church in Christ, outside the Church, . . . faith loses its "measure"; it no longer finds its equilibrium, the space needed to sustain itself. Faith is necessarily ecclesial; it is professed from within the body of Christ as a concrete communion of believers. It is against this ecclesial backdrop that faith opens the individual Christian toward all others.

Christ's word, once heard, by virtue of its inner power at work in the heart of the Christian, becomes a response, a spoken word, a profession of faith. As Saint Paul puts it: "One believes with the heart . . . and confesses with the lips" (Rom. 10:10).

31
Operative Faith

Faith becomes operative in the Christian on the basis of the gift received, the love that attracts our hearts to Christ (Gal. 5:6) and enables us to become part of the Church's great pilgrimage through history until the end of the world. For those who have been transformed in this way, a new way of seeing opens up; faith becomes light for their eyes.

Again, we turn to Saint Paul: "One believes with the heart . . . and confesses with the lips" (Rom. 10:10). Faith comes from hearing, and it is meant to find expression in words and to be proclaimed. For "how are they to believe in him of whom they have never heard? And how are they to hear without a preacher?" (Rom. 10:14).

32

Faith Is Not an Individual Decision

It is impossible to believe on our own. Faith is not simply an individual decision that takes place in the depths of the believer's heart; nor is it a completely private relationship between the "I" of the believer and the divine "Thou," between an autonomous subject and God. By its very nature, faith is open to the "We" of the Church; it always takes place within her communion.

We are reminded of this by the dialogical format of the creed used in the baptismal liturgy. Our belief is expressed in response to an invitation, to a word that must be heard and that is not our own; it exists as part of a dialogue and cannot be merely a profession originating in an individual. We can respond in the singular—"I believe"—only because we are part of a greater fellowship, only because we also say, "We believe."

33
Faith Reveals

Faith reveals just how firm the bonds between people can be when God is present in their midst. Faith does not merely grant interior firmness, a steadfast conviction on the part of the believer; it also sheds light on every human relationship because it is born of love and reflects God's own love. The God who is himself reliable gives us a city that is reliable.

Meanwhile, the Gospel tells us constantly to run the risk of a face-to-face encounter with others, with their physical presence, which challenges us, with their pain and their pleas, with their joy, which infects us in our close and continuous interaction. True faith in the incarnate Son of God is inseparable from self-giving, from membership in the community, from service, from reconciliation with others. The Son of God, by becoming flesh, summoned us to the revolution of tenderness.

34
Guarding the Faith

One aspect of the light that guides us on the journey of faith is holy "cunning." This holy cunning is also a virtue. It consists of a spiritual shrewdness that enables us to recognize danger and avoid it. The Magi used this light of cunning when, on the way back, they decided not to pass by the gloomy palace of Herod but to take another route. These wise men from the east teach us how not to fall into the snares of darkness and how to defend ourselves from the shadows that seek to envelop us. By this holy cunning, the Magi guarded the faith.

On the feast of the Epiphany, as we recall Jesus' manifestation to humanity in the face of a Child, may we sense the Magi at our side, as wise companions on the way. Their example helps us to lift our gaze toward the star and to follow the great desires of our heart. They teach us not to be content with a life of mediocrity, of "playing it safe," but to let ourselves be attracted always by what is good, true, and beautiful.

35

"Cunning" Faith

We, too, need to guard the faith, guard it from darkness. Many times, however, it is a darkness under the guise of light. This is because the devil, as Saint Paul says, disguises himself at times as an angel of light. And this is where a holy "cunning" is necessary to protect the faith. . . .

Faith, though, is also a grace; it is a gift. We are entrusted with the task of guarding it by means of this holy cunning and by prayer, love, and charity. We need to welcome the light of God into our hearts and, at the same time, cultivate that spiritual cunning that is able to combine simplicity with astuteness, as Jesus told his disciples: "Be wise as serpents and innocent as doves" (Matt. 10:16).

36
Faith Transforms

Faith transforms the whole person precisely to the extent that he or she becomes open to love. Through this blending of faith and love, we come to see the kind of knowledge that faith entails, its power to convince and its ability to illumine our steps. Faith knows because it is tied to love, because love itself brings enlightenment. Faith's understanding is born when we receive the immense love of God, which transforms us inwardly and enables us to see reality with new eyes.

All of us are called to offer others an explicit witness to the saving love of the Lord, who, despite our imperfections, offers us his closeness, his word, and his strength, and gives meaning to our lives. In your heart, you know that it is not the same to live without him; what you have come to realize, what has helped you to live and given you hope, is what you also need to communicate to others.

37

The Witness of Faith

Our falling short of perfection should be no excuse; on the contrary, mission is a constant stimulus not to remain mired in mediocrity but to continue growing. The witness of faith to which each Christian is called leads us to say with Saint Paul: "Not that I have already obtained this, or am already perfect; but I press on to make it my own, because Christ Jesus has made me his own" (Phil. 3:12).

When we live out a spirituality of drawing nearer to others and seeking their welfare, our hearts are opened wide to the Lord's greatest and most beautiful gifts. Whenever we encounter another person in love, we learn something new about God. Whenever our eyes are opened to acknowledge the other, we grow in the light of faith and knowledge of God.

38
Having Faith

What can I, a weak, fragile sinner, do? Well, God says to you: do not be afraid of holiness; do not be afraid to aim high, to let yourself be loved and purified by God; do not be afraid to let yourself be guided by the Holy Spirit. Let us be infected by the holiness of God. Every Christian is called to sanctity, and sanctity does not consist especially in doing extraordinary things but in allowing God to act. It is the meeting of our weakness with the strength of his grace, it is having faith in his action that allows us to live in charity, to do everything with joy and humility, for the glory of God and as a service to our neighbor.

There is a celebrated saying by the French writer Léon Bloy, who, in the last moments of his life, said: "The only real sadness in life is not becoming a saint." Let us not lose the hope of holiness; let us follow this path. Do we want to be saints? The Lord awaits us, with open arms; he waits to accompany us on the path to sanctity. Let us live in the joy of our faith, let us allow ourselves to be loved by the Lord, and let us ask for this gift from God in prayer—for ourselves and for others.

39
Faith and Doubt

I think that some of you might ask me: "Father, but I have many doubts about the faith; what should I do? Don't you ever have doubts?" I have many, of course; everyone has doubts at times! Doubts that touch the faith, in a positive way, are a sign that we want to know better and more fully God, Jesus, and the mystery of his love for us. "Still, I have this doubt: I seek, I study, I consult or ask advice about what to do." These are doubts that bring about growth! It is good, therefore, that we ask questions about our faith, because in this way we are pushed to deepen it.

Doubts, however, must also be overcome. For this, it is necessary to listen to the Word of God and to understand what he teaches us. An important path that really helps with this is *catechesis*, in which the proclamation of the faith is encountered in the concreteness of individual and community life. And there is, at the same time, another equally important path, that of *living* the faith as much as possible.

40
Faith Is Fidelity

Let us not make of faith an abstract theory in which doubts multiply. Rather, let us make of faith our life. Let us seek to practice it in service to our brothers and sisters, especially those who are most in need. And thus many doubts disappear, because we feel the presence of God and the truth of the Gospel in love, which—without our deserving it—lives in us, and we share it with others.

I ask myself: Am I a Christian by fits and starts, or am I a Christian full time? Our culture of the ephemeral, the relative, also takes its toll on the way we live our faith. God asks us to be faithful to him, daily, in our everyday life. He goes on to say that, even if we are sometimes unfaithful to him, he remains faithful. In his mercy, he never tires of stretching out his hand to lift us up, to encourage us to continue our journey and to come back and tell him of our weakness, so that he can grant us his strength. This is the real journey: to walk with the Lord always, even at moments of weakness, even in our sins. Never to prefer a makeshift path of our own. Faith is ultimate fidelity, like that of Mary.

41

Faith-Knowledge

Faith-knowledge, because it is born of God's covenantal love, is knowledge that lights up a path in history. That is why, in the Bible, truth and fidelity go together: the true God is the God of fidelity who keeps his promises and makes possible, in time, a deeper understanding of his plan. . . .

Faith-knowledge sheds light not only on the destiny of one particular people but also on the entire history of the created world, from its origins to its consummation.

42
Keeping the Faith

Today, this is of vital importance: to keep the faith. We must press on further, beyond the darkness, beyond the voices that raise alarm, beyond worldliness, beyond so many forms of modernity that exist today. We must press on toward Bethlehem, where, in the simplicity of a dwelling on the outskirts, beside a mother and father full of love and faith, there shines forth the Sun from on high, the King of the universe. By the example of the Magi, with our little lights, may we seek the Light and keep the faith. May it be so.

43

The Obedience of Faith

Knowledge linked to a word is always personal knowledge; it recognizes the voice of the one speaking, opens up to that person in freedom, and follows him or her in obedience. Saint Paul could thus speak of the "obedience of faith." Faith is also a knowledge bound to the passage of time, for words take time to be pronounced, and it is a knowledge assimilated only along a journey of discipleship. The experience of hearing can thus help bring out more clearly the bond between knowledge and love.

The truth that faith discloses to us is a truth centered on an encounter with Christ, on the contemplation of his life, and on the awareness of his presence.

44
Right Faith

Right faith orients reason to open itself to the light that comes from God, so that reason, guided by love of the truth, can come to a deeper knowledge of God. The great medieval theologians and teachers rightly held that theology, as a science of faith, is a participation in God's own knowledge of himself. It is not just our discourse about God but is first and foremost the acceptance and the pursuit of a deeper understanding of the word God speaks to us, the word God speaks about himself, for he is an eternal dialogue of communion, and he allows us to enter this dialogue.

Theology thus demands the humility to be touched by God, admitting its own limitations before the mystery while striving to investigate, with the discipline proper to reason, the inexhaustible riches of this mystery.

45

Faith Awakens

Nor is the light of faith, joined to the truth of love, extraneous to the material world, for love is always lived out in body and spirit; the light of faith is an incarnate light radiating from the luminous life of Jesus. It also illumines the material world, trusts its inherent order, and knows that it calls us to an ever-widening path of harmony and understanding.

The gaze of science thus benefits from faith: faith encourages the scientist to remain constantly open to reality in all its inexhaustible richness. Faith awakens the critical sense by preventing research from being satisfied with its own formulas and helps it realize that nature is always greater. By stimulating wonder before the profound mystery of creation, faith broadens the horizons of reason to shed greater light on the world, which discloses itself to scientific investigation.

46

Faith and Reason

Faith is not fearful of reason; on the contrary, it seeks and trusts reason, since "the light of reason and the light of faith both come from God" (Saint Thomas Aquinas) and cannot contradict each other. Evangelization is attentive to scientific advances and wishes to shed on them the light of faith . . . so that they will remain respectful of the . . . supreme value of the human person at every stage of life. All society can be enriched by this dialogue, which opens new horizons for thought and expands the possibilities of reason. This is a path of harmony and peace.

The Church has no wish to hold back the marvelous progress of science. On the contrary, she rejoices and even delights in acknowledging the enormous potential that God has given to the human mind. Whenever the sciences—rigorously focused on their specific fields of inquiry—arrive at a conclusion that reason cannot refute, faith does not contradict it.

Neither can believers claim that a scientific opinion that is attractive but not sufficiently verified has the same weight as a dogma of faith. At times, some scientists have exceeded the limits of their scientific competence by making certain statements or claims. But here the problem is not with reason itself but with the promotion of a particular ideology, which blocks the path to authentic, serene, and productive dialogue.

47
Faith and Sacraments

Our faith is not an abstract doctrine or philosophy but a vital and full relationship with a person: Jesus Christ, the only-begotten Son of God, who became man, was put to death, rose from the dead to save us, and is now living in our midst. Where can we encounter him? We encounter him in the Church, in our hierarchical Holy Mother Church. It is the Church that says today: "Behold the Lamb of God"; it is the Church that proclaims him; it is in the Church that Jesus continues to accomplish his acts of grace, which are the sacraments.

The sacraments communicate an incarnate memory, linked to the times and places of our lives, linked to all our senses; in them the whole person is engaged as a member of a living subject and part of a network of communitarian relationships. While the sacraments are indeed sacraments of faith, it can also be said that faith itself possesses a sacramental structure. The awakening of faith is linked to the dawning of a new sacramental sense in our lives as human beings and as Christians, in which visible and material realities are seen to point beyond themselves to the mystery of the eternal.

48
The Faith of the Church

Baptism integrates us into the body of the Church, into the holy People of God. And in this body, in this people journeying on, faith is passed down from generation to generation: It is the faith of the Church. It is the faith of Mary, our mother, the faith of Saint Joseph, of Saint Peter, of Saint Paul, of Saint Andrew, and of Saint John. It is the faith of the apostles and of the martyrs, which has come down to us through baptism: the chain of transmission of the faith. This is really beautiful.

49

Faith Is Light

Faith is light: in the ceremony of baptism, you will be given a lighted candle, as in the early days of the Church. In those days, baptism was called "illumination" because faith illuminates the heart; it shows things in a different light. You have asked for faith, and the Church gives faith to your children with baptism, and you have the task of making it grow, safeguarding it, so that it may become testimony for all others. This is the meaning of this ceremony. I would like to tell you only this: safeguard the faith; make it grow, so it may be testimony for others.

Baptism makes us see, then, that faith is not the achievement of isolated individuals; it is not an act someone can perform on his or her own, but rather something that must be received by entering into the ecclesial communion, which transmits God's gift. No one baptizes himself or herself, just as no one comes into the world [alone]. Baptism is something we receive.

50

The Sacraments: Gifts of Faith

The structure of baptism demonstrates the critical importance of cooperation between Church and family in passing on the faith. Parents are called, as Saint Augustine once said, not only to bring children into the world but also to bring them to God, so that through baptism they can be reborn as children of God and receive the gift of faith. Thus, along with life, children are given a fundamental orientation and assured of a good future; this orientation will be further strengthened in the sacrament of confirmation with the seal of the Holy Spirit.

The Eucharist is an act of remembrance, a making present of the mystery in which the past, as an event of death and resurrection, demonstrates its ability to open up a future, to foreshadow ultimate fulfillment. In the Eucharist we learn to see the heights and depths of reality. The bread and wine [become] the body and blood of Christ, who becomes present in his passover to the Father. This movement draws us, body and soul, into the movement of all creation toward its fulfillment in God.

51
Joyful Faith

The grace of the sacraments nourishes in us a strong and joyful faith, a faith that knows how to stand in wonder before the marvels of God and knows how to resist the idols of the world. That is why it is important to take communion. It is important that children be baptized early, that they be confirmed, because the sacraments are the presence of Jesus Christ in us, a presence that helps us.

52

God's Faithful Love

Every human person is called to encounter the Lord in his or her life. Christian faith is a gift that we receive in baptism and that allows us to encounter God. Faith intersects times of joy and pain, of light and darkness, as in every authentic experience of love. . . .

May the Virgin Mary, model of meditation of the words and acts of the Lord, help us rediscover with faith the beauty and richness of the Eucharist and the other sacraments, which render present God's faithful love for us. In this way we fall ever more in love with the Lord Jesus, our bridegroom, and we go to meet him with our lamps alight with our joyous faith, thus becoming his witnesses in the world.

53
The Life of Faith

The life of faith consists in the wish to abide in the Lord and thus in a continuing search for the place where he lives. This means that we are called to surpass a methodical and predictable religiosity, rekindling the encounter with Jesus in prayer, in meditating on the Word of God, and in practicing the sacraments, to abide with him and bear fruit thanks to him, his help, and his grace.

On the eve of his passion, Jesus gave himself to his apostles under the signs of bread and wine. In the gift of the Eucharist, we not only recognize, with the eyes of faith, the gift of his body and blood; we also learn how to *rest in his wounds* and there to be cleansed of all our sins and foolish ways. By taking refuge in Christ's wounds, may we know the healing balm of the Father's mercy and find the strength to bring it to others, to anoint every hurt and every painful memory. In this way, you will be faithful witnesses to the reconciliation and peace that God wants to reign in every human heart and in every community.

54

Professing Our Faith

The believer who professes his or her faith is taken up, as it were, into the truth being professed. He or she cannot truthfully recite the words of the creed without being changed, without becoming part of that history of love that embraces us and expands our being, making it part of a great fellowship . . . namely, the Church. All the truths in which we believe point to the mystery of the new life of faith as a journey of communion with the living God.

Faith also means believing in God, believing that he truly loves us, that he is alive, that he is mysteriously capable of intervening, that he does not abandon us, and that he brings good out of evil by his power and his infinite creativity. It means believing that he marches triumphantly in history with those who "are called and chosen and faithful" (Rev. 17:14).

55

An Attitude of Faith

With an attitude of faith, we can also understand the meaning of the "Bread of Life" that Jesus gives us, which he describes in this way: "I am the living bread which came down from heaven; if any one eats of this bread, he will live for ever; and the bread which I shall give for the life of the world is my flesh" (John 6:51, 56–58). In Jesus, in his "flesh"—that is, in his concrete humanity—is all the love of God, which is the Holy Spirit. Those who let themselves be drawn by this love go to Jesus and go with faith, and they receive from him life, eternal life.

56

Faith and Creation

Faith, by revealing the love of God the Creator, enables us to respect nature all the more and to discern in it a grammar written by the hand of God and a dwelling place entrusted to our protection and care.

Faith also helps us devise models of development that are based not simply on utility and profit but consider creation as a gift for which we are all indebted; it teaches us to create just forms of government, in the realization that authority comes from God and is meant for the service of the common good.

57

Faith and Forgiveness

Faith offers the possibility of forgiveness, which so often demands time and effort, patience and commitment. Forgiveness is possible once we discover that goodness is always prior to and more powerful than evil and that the word with which God affirms our life is deeper than our every denial. From a purely anthropological standpoint, unity is superior to conflict; rather than avoiding conflict, we need to confront it in an effort to resolve and move beyond it, to make it a link in a chain, as part of progress toward unity.

Whether believers or not, we are agreed today that the earth is essentially a shared inheritance, whose fruits are meant to benefit everyone. For believers, this becomes a question of fidelity to the Creator because God created the world for everyone. Hence, every ecological approach needs to incorporate a social perspective that takes into account the fundamental rights of the poor and the underprivileged. The principle of the subordination of private property to the universal destination of goods, and thus the right of everyone to their use, is a golden rule of social conduct and "the first principle of the whole ethical and social order" (Saint John Paul II, encyclical letter *Laborem Exercens*, September 14, 1981).

58

Consonant with Our Faith

Believers themselves must constantly feel challenged to live in a way consonant with their faith and not to contradict it by their actions. They need to be encouraged to be ever open to God's grace and to draw constantly from their deepest convictions about love, justice, and peace.

If a mistaken understanding of our own principles has at times led us to justify mistreating nature, to exercise tyranny over creation, to engage in war, injustice, and acts of violence, then we believers should acknowledge that, by so doing, we were not faithful to the treasures of wisdom we have been called to protect and preserve.

59

Faith and Responsibility

As believers, we do not look at the world from without but from within, conscious of the bonds with which the Father has linked us to all beings. By developing our individual, God-given capacities, an ecological conversion can inspire us to greater creativity and enthusiasm in resolving the world's problems and in offering ourselves to God.

We do not understand our superiority as a reason for personal glory or irresponsible dominion but rather as a different capacity that, in its turn, entails a serious responsibility stemming from our faith.

60

Faith in Public Life

In the letter to the Hebrews, we read that "God is not ashamed to be called their God; indeed, he has prepared a city for them." Here, the expression "is not ashamed" is associated with public acknowledgment. The intention is to say that God, by his concrete actions, makes a public avowal that he is present in our midst and that he desires to solidify every human relationship. Could it be the case, instead, that we are the ones who are ashamed to call God our God? That we are the ones who fail to confess him as such in our public life, who fail to propose the grandeur of the life in common that he makes possible?

When faith is weakened, the foundations of public life also risk being weakened. . . . If we remove faith in God from our cities, mutual trust would be weakened, we would remain united only by fear, and our stability would be threatened.

61

Faith Illumines Life and Society

Faith illumines life and society. If it possesses a creative light for each new moment of history, it is because it sets every event in relationship to the origin and destiny of all things in the Father.

The faith is nowadays being challenged by the proliferation of new religious movements, some of which tend to fundamentalism while others seem to propose a spirituality without God. This is, on the one hand, a human reaction to a materialistic, consumerist, and individualistic society, but it is also a means of exploiting the weaknesses of people living in poverty and on the fringes of society, people who make ends meet amid great human suffering and are looking for immediate solutions to their needs.

Today, our challenge is not so much atheism as the need to respond adequately to many people's thirst for God, lest they try to satisfy it with alienating solutions or with a disembodied Jesus who demands nothing of us with regard to others. Unless these people find in the Church a spirituality that can offer healing and liberation and fill them with life and peace, while at the same time summoning them to fraternal communion and missionary fruitfulness, they will end up being taken in by solutions that neither make life truly human nor give glory to God.

62
Faith and Suffering

Faith, even when it is as tiny as a grain of mustard seed, can move mountains. How many times has the power of faith enabled us to utter the word *pardon* in humanly impossible situations. People who have suffered violence and abuse, either themselves, or in the person of their loved ones, or their property, know there are some wounds that only God's power, his mercy, can heal.

When violence is met with forgiveness, even the hearts of those who have done wrong can be conquered by the love that triumphs over every form of evil. In this way, among the victims and among those who wronged them, God raises up true witnesses and workers of mercy.

63

Faith Is Hope

Faith is not a light that scatters all our darkness but a lamp that guides our steps in the night and suffices for the journey. To those who suffer, God does not provide arguments that explain everything; rather, his response is that of an accompanying presence, a history of goodness that touches every story of suffering and opens up a ray of light. In Christ, God himself wishes to share this path with us and to offer us his gaze so that we might see the light within it. Christ is the one who, having endured suffering, is "the pioneer and perfecter of our faith" (Heb.12:2).

Suffering reminds us that faith's service to the common good is always one of hope, a hope that looks ever ahead in the knowledge that only from God, from the future that comes from the risen Jesus, can our society find solid and lasting foundations. In this sense, faith is linked to hope, for even if our dwelling place here below is wasting away, we have an eternal dwelling place, which God has already prepared in Christ, in his body.

64

The Flame of Faith in Darkness

The darkness of death should be confronted with a more intense work of love. "My God, lighten my darkness!" is the invocation of evening prayer. In the light of the resurrection of the Lord, who abandons none of those whom the Father entrusted to him, we can take the sting out of death, as Saint Paul says; we can prevent it from poisoning life, from rendering vain our love, or from pushing us into the darkest chasm.

We are all small and defenseless before the mystery of death. However, what a grace if, at that moment, we safeguard in our heart the little flame of faith! Jesus takes us by the hand, as he took Jairus's daughter by the hand, and repeats once again: "Talitha cumi"; "Little girl, arise!" He will say this to each one of us: "Arise, rise again!"

I invite you to close your eyes and think about that moment: the moment of our death. And imagine that moment that will come, when Jesus will take us by the hand and say: "Come, come with me, arise."

65

Humble Faith

How does the Lord challenge us when he speaks of faith? He says, "If you had faith as a grain of mustard seed, you could say to this sycamine tree, 'Be rooted up, and be planted in the sea,' and it would obey you" (Luke 17:5–6). A mustard seed is tiny, yet Jesus says that faith this size, small but true and sincere, suffices to achieve what is humanly impossible, unthinkable. And it is true. We all know people who are simple, humble, but whose faith is so strong it can move mountains.

Let us think, for example, of some mothers and fathers who face very difficult situations, or of some sick, and even gravely ill, people who transmit serenity to those who come to visit them. These people, because of their faith, do not boast about what they do; rather, as Jesus asks in the Gospel, they say, "We are unworthy servants; we have only done what was our duty" (Luke 17:10). How many people among us have such strong, humble faith, and what good they do!

66
Mary's Faith

The silent witness to the events of Jesus' passion and resurrection was Mary. She stood beside the cross: she did not fold in the face of pain; her faith made her strong. In the broken heart of the mother, the flame of hope was kept ever burning.

Let us ask her to help us, too, to fully accept the proclamation of the Resurrection, so as to embody it in the concreteness of our daily lives. May the Virgin Mary give us the faithful certitude that every step suffered on our journey, illuminated by the light of Easter, will become a blessing and a joy for us and for others, especially for those suffering because of selfishness and indifference.

67

Mary as the Model of Our Faith

In what sense does Mary represent a model for the Church's faith? Let us think about who the Virgin Mary was: a Jewish girl who was waiting with all her heart for the redemption of her people. But in the heart of the young daughter of Israel there was a secret that even she herself did not yet know: in God's loving plan, she was destined to become the mother of the Redeemer.

In Mary, the Daughter of Zion, is fulfilled the long history of faith of the Old Testament, with its account of so many faithful women, beginning with Sarah—women who, alongside the patriarchs, were those in whom God's promise was fulfilled and new life flowered. In the fullness of time, God's word was spoken to Mary, and she received that word into her heart, her entire being, so that in her womb it could take flesh and be born as light for humanity.

68

Mary, Faith Demonstrated

In the mother of Jesus, faith demonstrated its fruitfulness; when our own spiritual lives bear fruit, we become filled with joy, which is the clearest sign of faith's grandeur. In her own life, Mary completed the pilgrimage of faith, following in the footsteps of her Son. In her, the faith journey of the Old Testament was thus taken up into the following of Christ, [of being] transformed by him, and of entering the gaze of the incarnate Son of God.

But Mary's true motherhood also ensured for the Son of God an authentic human history, true flesh in which he would die on the cross and rise from the dead. Mary would accompany Jesus to the cross, whence her motherhood would extend to each of his disciples. She will also be present in the upper room after Jesus' resurrection and ascension, joining the apostles in imploring the gift of the Spirit.

69

Illumined by the Faith of Mary

Mary herself experienced these things during the years of Jesus' childhood in Nazareth. This is the beginning of the Gospel, the joyful good news. However, it is not difficult to see in that beginning a particular heaviness of heart, linked with a sort of night of faith—to use the words of Saint John of the Cross—a kind of veil through which one has to draw near to the Invisible One and to live in intimacy with the mystery. And this is the way that Mary, for many years, lived in intimacy with the mystery of her Son and went forward in her pilgrimage of faith.

We can ask ourselves a question: Do we allow ourselves to be illumined by the faith of Mary, who is our mother? Or do we think of her as distant, as someone too different from us? In moments of difficulty, trial, and darkness, do we look to her as a model of trust in God, who always and only desires our good? Let's think about this: perhaps it will do us good to rediscover Mary as the model and figure of the Church in this faith that she possessed.

70

The Faith of Our Mother

Mary's faith begins with an attitude of faith, which consists in listening to the Word of God to abandon herself to this Word with full willingness of mind and heart. Responding to the angel, Mary said: "Behold, I am the handmaid of the Lord; let it be to me according to your word" (Luke 1:38). In her "behold," filled with faith, Mary does not know by what road she must venture, what pains she must suffer, or what risks she must face. But she is aware that it is the Lord asking, and she entrusts herself totally to him; she abandons herself to his love. This is the faith of Mary.

The Gospel shows us the truest cause of Mary's greatness and her blessedness: faith. Indeed, Elizabeth greets her with these words: "Blessed is she who believed that there would be a fulfillment of what was spoken to her from the Lord" (Luke 1:45). Faith is the heart of Mary's whole story: she is the believer, the great believer. She knows—and she says so—that, historically, the violence of the powerful, the pride of the rich, and the arrogance of the proud are burdensome. However, Mary believes and proclaims that God does not leave his humble and poor children alone but helps them with mercy, with care, overthrowing the mighty from their thrones, scattering the proud in the machinations of their hearts. This is the faith of our mother; this is the faith of Mary.

71

Mary's Merciful Faith

Mary is the model of virtue and of faith. In contemplating her assumption into heaven, the final fulfillment of her earthly journey, we thank her because she always precedes us in the pilgrimage of life and faith. She is the first disciple. And we ask her to keep us and support us, that we may have a strong, joyful, and merciful faith and that she may help us to be saints, to meet with her, one day, in heaven.

But Mary's motherhood is not reduced to this: thanks to her faith, she is also the first disciple of Jesus and this expands her motherhood. It will be Mary's faith that provokes the first miraculous sign in Cana, which contributes to [the increase in] the disciples' faith. With the same faith, Mary is present at the foot of the cross and receives the apostle John as her son. And, lastly, after the Resurrection, she becomes the prayerful mother of the Church on which the power of the Holy Spirit descends on the day of Pentecost.

72
Mary's Pilgrimage of Faith

Mary said her "yes" to God: a "yes" that threw her simple life in Nazareth into turmoil, and not only once. Any number of times she had to utter a heartfelt "yes" at moments of joy and sorrow, culminating in the "yes" she spoke at the foot of the Cross. Think of the full extent of Mary's faithfulness to God: seeing her only Son hanging on the Cross. The faithful woman, still standing, utterly heartbroken, yet faithful and strong.

Mary has always been present in the hearts, the piety, and, above all, the pilgrimage of faith of the Christian people. "The Church journeys through time . . . and on this journey she proceeds along the path already trodden by the Virgin Mary" (*Redemptoris Mater,* 2).

Our journey of faith is the same as that of Mary, and so we feel that she is particularly close to us. As far as faith, the hinge of the Christian life, is concerned, the Mother of God shared our condition. She had to take the same path as we do, a path that is sometimes difficult and obscure. She had to advance in the "pilgrimage of faith" (*Lumen gentium,* 58).

73

Faith Unfailing

Our pilgrimage of faith has been inseparably linked to Mary ever since Jesus, dying on the Cross, gave her to us as our mother, saying: "Behold your mother!" (John 19:27). These words serve as a testament, bequeathing to the world a mother. From that moment on, the Mother of God also became our mother. When the faith of the disciples was most tested by difficulties and uncertainties, Jesus entrusted them to Mary, who was the first to believe and whose faith would never fail. The "woman" became our mother when she lost her divine Son. Her sorrowing heart was enlarged to make room for all men and women—all, whether good or bad—and she loves them all, as she loved Jesus.

74
Family and Faith

Psalm 78 celebrates the proclamation of faith within families: "All that we have heard and known, / that our fathers have told us, / we will not hide from their children, / but tell to the coming generation / the glorious deeds of the Lord, and his might, / and the wonders which he has wrought. / He established a testimony in Jacob, / and appointed a law in Israel, / which he commanded our fathers to teach to their children; / that the next generation might know them, / the children yet unborn, / and arise and tell them to their children."

The family is thus the place where parents become their children's first teachers in the faith. They learn this "trade," passing it down from one person to another: "When in time to come your son asks you . . . You shall say to him . . . " (Ex. 13:14). Thus succeeding generations can raise their song to the Lord: "Young men and maidens together, old and young together!" (Ps. 148:12).

75

Faith Is God's Gift

Raising children calls for an orderly process of handing on the faith. This is made difficult by current lifestyles, work schedules, and the complexity of today's world, in which many people keep up a frenetic pace just to survive. Even so, the home must continue to be the place where we learn to appreciate the meaning and beauty of the faith, to pray and to serve our neighbor. This begins with baptism, in which, as Saint Augustine said, mothers who bring their children "cooperate in the sacred birthing" and begin the journey of growth in that new life.

Faith is God's gift, received in baptism, and not our own work, yet parents are the means that God uses for it to grow and develop. . . . Handing on the faith presumes that parents themselves genuinely trust God, seek him, and sense their need for him, for only in this way does "one generation laud your works to another, and declare your mighty acts" (Ps. 145:4) and "fathers make known to children your faithfulness" (Isa. 38:19).

76
Education and Faith

Education in the faith must adapt to each child, because older resources and recipes do not always work. Children need symbols, actions, and stories. Since adolescents usually have issues with authority and rules, it is best to encourage their own experience of faith and to provide them with attractive testimonies that win them over by their sheer beauty.

Parents who desire to nurture the faith of their children are sensitive to their patterns of growth, for they know that spiritual experience is not imposed but freely proposed. It is essential that children actually see that, for their parents, prayer is something truly important. Hence, moments of family prayer and acts of devotion can be more powerful for evangelization than any catechism class or sermon.

77

Families and Faith

We can ask: How do we keep our faith as a family? Do we keep it for ourselves, in our families, as a personal treasure like a bank account? Or are we able to share it by our witness, by our acceptance of others, by our openness? We all know that families, especially young families, are often "racing" from one place to another, with lots to do. But did you ever think that this racing could also be the race of faith?

And thanks to faith we have been begotten by God. This is what happens at *baptism*. We have heard the apostle John: "Everyone who believes that Jesus is the Christ is a child of God" (1 John 5:1). Your children are baptized in this faith. Today it is *your* faith, dear parents, godfathers, and godmothers. It is the faith of the Church, in which these little ones receive baptism. But tomorrow, by the grace of God, it will be *their* faith, their personal "yes" to Jesus Christ, which gives us the Father's love.

78

Transmission of the Faith

How do we live God's faithful love toward us? There is always the risk of forgetting the great love that the Lord has shown us. Even we Christians run the risk of letting ourselves be paralyzed by fears of the future and looking for security in things that pass or in a model of a closed society that tends to exclude more than include. . . .

In the footsteps of the saints, we, too, can live the joy of the Gospel by practicing mercy; we can share the difficulties of so many people—of families, especially those who are weakest and marked by the economic crisis. Families need to feel the Church's motherly caress to go forward in married life, in the upbringing of children, in the care of the elderly, and also in the transmission of the faith to the younger generations.

79

Faith Opens a Window

Faith opens a "window" to the presence and working of the Spirit. It shows us that, like happiness, holiness is always tied to little gestures. "Whoever gives you a cup of water in my name will not go unrewarded," Jesus says in Mark 9:41. These little gestures are those we learn at home, in the family; they get lost amid all the other things we do, yet they do make each day different. They are the quiet things done by mothers and grandmothers, by fathers and grandfathers, by children, by brothers and sisters. They are little signs of tenderness, affection, and compassion. Such as the warm supper we look forward to at night, the early lunch awaiting someone who is going to work. Small gestures. Like a blessing before we go to bed, or a hug after we return from a hard day's work. Love is shown by little things, by attention to small daily signs that make us feel at home. Faith grows when it is lived and shaped by love. That is why our families, our homes, are true domestic churches. They are the right place for faith to become life, and life to grow in faith.

80
The Dialect of Faith

I would like to tell you only one thing: first transmission of the faith can be done only in dialect of the family, in the dialect of daddy and mommy, of grandpa and grandma. Then the catechists will come to develop this first transmission, with ideas and explanations. But do not forget this: it is done in dialect, and if the dialect is missing—if at home that language of love is not spoken between the parents—then the transmission is not very easy; it cannot be done. Do not forget. Your task is to transmit the faith but to do so with the dialect of love of your home, of your family.

81
"If you *had* faith . . ."

To have faith, a lively faith, it is not easy; and so, we pass to the second request the apostles bring to the Lord in the Gospel: "Increase our faith!" (Luke 17:6). It is a good request, a prayer that we, too, can direct to the Lord each day. But the divine response is surprising and turns the question around: "If you *had* faith . . ." (Luke 17:6). It is the Lord who asks us to have faith. Because faith, which is always God's gift and always to be asked for, must be nurtured by us.

82

A Faith That Nourishes

It is prayer that conserves the faith; without it, faith falters. Let us ask the Lord for a faith that is incessant prayer, persevering, like that of the widow in the parable, a faith that nourishes our desire for his coming. And in prayer let us experience that compassion of God, who, like a Father, comes to encounter his children, full of merciful love.

83
The Breath of Faith Is Prayer

Each one of us can testify to Christ by the power of faith. The faith we have is miniscule, but it is strong. . . . And how do we draw from this strength? We draw it from God in prayer. Prayer is the breath of faith: in a relationship of trust, in a relationship of love, dialogue cannot be left out, and prayer is the dialogue of the soul with God.

God invites us to pray insistently, not because he is unaware of our needs or because he is not listening to us. On the contrary, he is always listening, and he knows everything about us lovingly. On our daily journey, especially in times of difficulty, in the battle against the evil that is outside and within us, the Lord is not far away; he is by our side. We battle with him beside us, and our weapon is prayer, which makes us feel his presence, his mercy, and his help.

84
With God Who Is Faithful

The battle against evil is a long and hard one; it requires patience and endurance, as when Moses had to keep his arms outstretched for the people to prevail. This is how it is: there is a battle to be waged each day, but God is our ally. Faith in him is our strength, and prayer is the expression of this faith. Therefore, Jesus assures us of the victory, but at the end he asks: "When the Son of man comes, will he find faith on earth?" (Luke 18:8). If faith is snuffed out, prayer is snuffed out, and we walk in the dark. We become lost on the path of life.

No Christian can go forward without being supported by persistent prayer. Prayer is the encounter with God: with God who never lets us down; with God who is faithful to his word; with God who does not abandon his children. Jesus asked, "And will not God vindicate his elect, who cry to him day and night?" (Luke 18:7). In prayer, believers express their faith and their trust, and God reveals his closeness.

85

A Fragile Faith

In Matthew 14 we find the account of Jesus walking on the water of the lake. After the multiplication of loaves and fish, he asks the disciples to get into the boat and go before him to the other side of the lake while he dismisses the crowds. He then goes up into the hills by himself to pray until late at night. Meanwhile, a strong storm blows up on the lake, and, right in the middle of the storm, Jesus reaches the disciples' boat, walking upon the water of the lake. When they see him, the disciples are terrified, but he calms them down, saying: "Take heart, it is I; have no fear!"

Peter, with his usual passion, practically puts him to the test: "Lord, if it is you, bid me come to you on the water," and Jesus answers, "Come!" Peter gets out of the boat and walks on the water; but a strong wind hits him, and he begins to sink. And so, he yells: "Lord, save me!" and Jesus reaches out his hand and catches him. . . . Peter, however, begins to sink the moment he looks away from Jesus, and he allows himself to be overwhelmed by the [waves]. But the Lord is always there, and when Peter calls him, Jesus saves him from danger. Peter, with his passion and weaknesses, can describe our faith: ever fragile and impoverished, anxious yet victorious, Christian faith walks to meet the risen Lord, amid the world's storms and dangers.

86

Of "Little Faith"

This is a beautiful story of the faith of the apostle Peter. In the voice of Jesus, who tells him, "Come!" he recognizes the echo of the first encounter on the shore of that very lake, and right away, once again, he leaves the boat and goes toward the Teacher. And he walks on the waters. The faithful and ready response to the Lord's call always enables one to achieve extraordinary things. But Jesus himself told us that we are capable of performing miracles with our faith: faith in him, faith in his word, faith in his voice. . . .

The final scene is very important. "And when they got into the boat, the wind ceased. And those in the boat worshipped him, saying, 'Truly you are the Son of God!'" All the disciples are on the boat, united in the experience of weakness, of doubt, of fear, and of "little faith." But when Jesus climbs into that boat again, the weather suddenly changes; they all feel united in their faith in him. All the little and frightened ones become great at the moment in which they fall on their knees and recognize the Son of God in their teacher. How many times the same thing happens to us. Without Jesus, [when we are] far from Jesus, we feel frightened and inadequate to the point of thinking we cannot succeed. Faith is lacking. But Jesus is always with us, hidden perhaps, but present and ready to support us.

87

A Genuine and Steadfast Faith

The story of Peter is an effective image of the Church: a boat that must brave the storms and sometimes seems on the point of capsizing. What saves her is not the skill and courage of her crew members but faith that allows her to [move forward], even in the dark, amid hardships. Faith gives us the certainty of Jesus' presence always beside us, of his hand that grasps us to pull us back from danger. We are all on this boat, and we feel secure here despite our limitations and weaknesses. We are especially safe when we are ready to kneel and worship Jesus, the only Lord of our life.

88

Upon This Faith

The Lord has in mind a picture of the structure, an image of the community like a building. This is why, when he hears Simon's candid profession of faith, he calls him a "rock" and declares his intention to build his Church upon this faith.

Jesus feels great joy in his heart because, in Simon, he recognizes the hand of the Father, the work of the Holy Spirit. He recognizes that God the Father has given Simon steadfast faith on which he, Jesus, can build his Church, meaning his community—that is, all of us. Jesus intends to give life to his Church, a people founded no longer on heritage but on *faith*, which means on the relationship with him, a relationship of love and trust. The Church is built on our relationship with Jesus. And to begin his Church, Jesus needs to find solid faith, steadfast faith in his disciples. And it is this that he must verify at this point of the journey.

89
A Sincere Faith

What happened in a unique way in Saint Peter also happens in every Christian who develops a sincere faith in Jesus the Christ, Son of the Living God. God asks each of us, is your faith good? Each one answers in his or her heart. Is my faith good? How does the Lord find our hearts? A heart that is firm as a rock, or a heart like sand, that is doubtful, diffident, disbelieving? It will do us good to think about this throughout the day today.

If the Lord finds [faith] in our heart—I don't say a perfect, but sincere, genuine faith—then he also sees in us living stones with which to build his community. This community's foundation stone is Christ, the unique cornerstone. On his side, Peter is the rock, the visible foundation of the Church's unity; but every baptized person is called to offer Jesus his or her lowly but sincere faith, so that he may continue to build his Church, today, in every part of the world.

90

To Strengthen Our Faith

The Lord does not turn away in the face of our needs, and if at times he seems insensitive to our requests for help, it is to test and strengthen our faith.

The Living God's love is a *faithful love, fidelity*: it is a love that does not disappoint; it never fails. Jesus embodies this love; he is the Witness. He never tires of loving us, of supporting us, of forgiving us, and thus he accompanies us on the path of life, according to the promise he made to the disciples: "I am with you always, to the close of the age" (Matt. 28:20). Out of love he became man, out of love he died and rose again, and out of love he is always at our side, in the beautiful moments and in the difficult ones.

91

The Courage of Faith

Jesus loves us always, until the end, without limits and without measure. And he loves us all, to the point that each one of us can say, "He gave his life for me." For me. Jesus' faithfulness does not fail, even in the face of our infidelity. Saint Paul reminds us of this: "If we are faithless, he remains faithful, for he cannot deny himself" (2 Tim. 2:13).

Finally, *the love of God is stable and secure*, as the rocky shores that provide shelter from the violence of the waves. Jesus manifests this in the miracle recounted in the Gospel, when he calms the storm, commanding the wind and the sea (Mark 4:41). The disciples are afraid because they realize that they will not make it, but he opens their hearts to the courage of faith. The Lord meets the man who shouts, "I can't do it anymore!" and offers the [firm foundation] of his love, to which everyone can cling, assured of not falling. How many times do we feel that we can't go on? But he is near us with his outstretched hand and open heart.

92
Ever Faithful

Do we believe that the Lord is faithful? How do we live the newness of God that transforms us every day? How do we live the steady love of the Lord that is placed as a secure barrier against the wakes of pride and false innovation? May the Holy Spirit help us always to be aware of this "rocky" love that makes us stable and strong in the small and great sufferings. May we not close ourselves off in the face of difficulties but to confront life with courage and look to the future with hope. As in the Sea of Galilee, today in the sea of our existence, Jesus overcomes the forces of evil and the threats of desperation. The peace that he gives us is for all.

Everything passes; only God remains. Indeed, kingdoms, peoples, cultures, nations, ideologies, and powers have passed, but the Church, founded on Christ, notwithstanding the many storms and our many sins, remains ever faithful to the deposit of faith shown in service. For the Church does not belong to popes, bishops, priests, nor the lay faithful; the Church in every moment belongs solely to Christ. Only the one who lives in Christ promotes and defends the Church by holiness of life, after the example of Peter and Paul.

93

Faith Is the Encounter with Jesus

Faith is born and reborn from a life-giving encounter with Jesus, from experiencing how his mercy illumines every situation in our lives. We would do well to renew this living encounter with the Lord each day. We would do well to read the word of God and in silent prayer to open our hearts to his love. We would do well to let our encounter with the Lord's tenderness enkindle joy in our hearts: a joy greater than sadness, a joy that even withstands pain and in turn becomes peace. All of this renews our life, makes us free and open to surprises, ready and available for the Lord and for others.

94
Faith in a Perfect Love

The word that God speaks to us in Jesus is not simply one word among many but is his eternal Word (Heb. 1:1–2). God can give no greater guarantee of his love, as Saint Paul reminds us (Rom. 8:31–39). Christian faith is thus faith in a perfect love, in its decisive power, in its ability to transform the world and to unfold its history. "We know and believe the love that God has for us" (1 John 4:16). In the love of God revealed in Jesus, faith perceives the foundation on which all reality and its final destiny rest.

95

The Dynamic of Faith

The word of the Lord astonishes us and makes us think. It introduces the *dynamic of faith*, which is a *relationship*: the relationship between the human person—each of us—and the person of Jesus, in which the Father plays a decisive role, and, of course, the Holy Spirit does too. To believe in him, it is not enough to meet Jesus, it is not enough to read the Bible, the Gospel—this is important. But it is not enough. It is not even enough to witness a miracle, such as that of the multiplication of the loaves. So many people were in close contact with Jesus and they did not believe. In fact, they even despised and condemned him. And I ask myself: Why this? Were they not attracted by the Father? No, this happened because their hearts were closed to the action of God's Spirit.

If your heart is closed, faith doesn't enter. Instead, God the Father draws us to Jesus: it is we who open or close our hearts. Instead, faith, which is like a seed deep in the heart, blossoms when we let the Father draw us to Jesus and we "go to him" with an open heart, without prejudices; then we recognize in his face the Face of God and in his words the Word of God, because the Holy Spirit has made us enter the relationship of love and of life between Jesus and God the Father. And there we receive a gift, the gift of the faith.

96

The Eyes of Faith

There are temptations for those who follow Jesus. None of the disciples stopped to attend to Bartimaeus, as Jesus did. They continued to walk, going on as if nothing were happening. If Bartimaeus was blind, they were deaf: his problem was not their problem. This can be a danger for us: in the face of constant problems, [we think] it is better to move on, instead of letting ourselves be bothered. In this way, just like the disciples, we are with Jesus, but we do not think like him. We are in his group, but our hearts are not open. We lose wonder, gratitude, and enthusiasm, and we risk becoming habitually unmoved by grace. We are able to speak about him and work for him, but we live far from his heart, which is reaching out to those who are wounded.

This is the temptation: a "spirituality of illusion." We walk through the deserts of humanity without seeing what is really there; instead, we see what we want to see. We are capable of developing views of the world, but we do not accept what the Lord places before our eyes. A faith that does not know how to root itself in the life of people remains arid, and rather than creating oases, it creates more deserts.

97

Resurrection Faith

Sacred Scripture itself contains *a path toward full faith in the resurrection of the dead*. This is expressed as faith in God as creator of the whole man, soul and body, and as faith in God the Liberator, the God who is faithful to the covenant with his people. In a vision, the prophet Ezekiel contemplates the graves of the exiled that are reopened, and whose dry bones come back to life thanks to the breath of a living spirit. This vision expresses hope in the future "resurrection of Israel"—that is, the rebirth of a people defeated and humiliated (Ez. 37:1–14).

Resurrection is not only the fact of rising after death but is also a new genre of life, which we already experience now. It is the victory over nothingness that we can already anticipate. Resurrection is the foundation of the faith and of Christian hope.

98

The Message of Faith

Were there no reference to paradise and to eternal life, Christianity would be reduced to ethics, to a philosophy of life. Instead, the message of Christian faith comes from heaven; it is revealed by God and goes beyond this world. Belief in resurrection is essential in order that our every act of Christian love not be ephemeral and an end in itself but may become a seed destined to blossom in the garden of God and to produce the fruit of eternal life.

Faith in the Resurrection is not a product of the Church; the Church herself is born of faith in the Resurrection. As Saint Paul says: "If Christ has not been raised, then our preaching is in vain and your faith is in vain" (1 Cor. 15:14).

99
Keeping the Faith

The apostle Paul, at the end of his life, makes a final reckoning and says: "I have kept the faith" (2 Tim. 4:7). But how did he keep the faith? Not hidden in a strong box. Nor did he hide it underground, as did the somewhat lazy servant. Saint Paul compares his life to a fight and to a race. He kept the faith because he didn't just defend it but proclaimed it, spread it, and brought it to distant lands. Saint Paul stood up to all those who wanted to preserve, to "embalm," the message of Christ within the limits of Palestine. That is why he made courageous decisions, he went into hostile territory, he let himself be challenged by distant peoples and different cultures, and he spoke frankly and fearlessly. Saint Paul kept the faith because, in the same way that he received it, he gave it away; he went out to the margins and didn't dig himself into defensive positions.

100
God Always Saves

Sometimes history, with its events and its protagonists, seems to go in the opposite direction of the plan of the heavenly Father, who wants justice, fraternity, and peace for all his children. But we are called to live these periods as seasons of trial, hope, and watchful waiting for the harvest.

Yesterday as today, the Kingdom of God grows in the world in a mysterious way, in a surprising way, revealing the hidden power of the small seed and its victorious vitality. Within the folds of personal and social events that sometimes seem to mark the shipwreck of hope, we must remain confident in the subdued but powerful action of God. This is why, in times of darkness and difficulty, we must not break down, we must keep the faith, and we must remain anchored in faithfulness to God, to his ever-saving presence. Remember this: God always saves.

Sources

1: Confessing Jesus
Homily, June 29, 2017
www.vatican.va

2: True Faith
Homily, April 29, 2017
www.vatican.va

3: Growing in Faith
Homily, April 29, 2017
www.vatican.va

4: By Faith
Interview by Antonio Spadaro, SJ, *America*, September 30, 2013
https://www.americamagazine.org/faith/2013/09/30/
big-heart-open-god-interview-pope-francis

5: A Faith That Calls Us by Name
Lumen Fidei, 8
www.vatican.va

6: Faith Is a Call and a Promise
Lumen Fidei, 9
www.vatican.va

7: Abraham's Faith
Lumen Fidei, 10
Lumen Fidei, 11
www.vatican.va

8: Faith Teaches
Lumen Fidei, 54
www.vatican.va

9: The Faith of Israel
Lumen Fidei, 14
www.vatican.va

10: Faith and the Decalogue
Lumen Fidei, 46
www.vatican.va

11: Biblical Faith
Lumen Fidei, 54
www.vatican.va

12: The Light of Faith
Lumen Fidei, 12
www.vatican.va

13: Faith Perceives
Lumen Fidei, 15
www.vatican.va

14: Faith and Remembrance
Homily, June 18, 2017
www.vatican.va

15: God's Gift of Faith
Lumen Fidei, 7
www.vatican.va

16: Christian Faith
Lumen Fidei, 15
www.vatican.va

17: Our Faith
Lumen Fidei, 18
www.vatican.va

18: The Touch of Faith
Lumen Fidei, 20
Lumen Fidei, 31
www.vatican.va

19: Faith Walking with Jesus
General Audience, October 16, 2013
www.vatican.va
Rite of Acceptance, November 23, 2013
www.vatican.va

20: Light of Faith
Lumen Fidei, 4
www.vatican.va

21: Faith, A Light for Our Darkness
Angelus, November 12, 2017
www.vatican.va
Lumen Fidei, 4
www.vatican.va

22: Faith in Jesus
Lumen Fidei, 35
Lumen Fidei, 13
www.vatican.va

23: Faith Is Passed On
Lumen Fidei, 37
www.vatican.va

24: The Lamp of Our Faith
Angelus, November 12, 2017
www.vatican.va

25: Faith in Idols
Lumen Fidei, 13
www.vatican.va

26: Faith, Tied to Conversion
Lumen Fidei, 13
www.vatican.va
General Audience, September 7, 2016
www.vatican.va
Lumen Fidei, 13
www.vatican.va

27: Faith, Turned in On Itself
General Audience, September 7, 2016
www.vatican.va

28: Real Faith Is Communal
Lumen Fidei, 22
www.vatican.va
Angelus, November 9, 2014
www.vatican.va

29: The Measure of Faith
Lumen Fidei, 22
www.vatican.va

30: The Profession of Faith
Lumen Fidei, 22
www.vatican.va

31: Operative Faith
Lumen Fidei, 22
www.vatican.va

32: Faith Is Not an Individual Decision
Lumen Fidei, 39
www.vatican.va

33: Faith Reveals
Lumen Fidei, 50
www.vatican.va
Evangelii Gaudium, 88
www.vatican.va

34: Guarding the Faith
Homily, January 6, 2014
www.vatican.va

35: "Cunning" Faith
Homily, January 6, 2014
www.vatican.va

36: Faith Transforms
Lumen Fidei, 26
www.vatican.va
Evangelii Gaudium, 121
www.vatican.va

37: The Witness of Faith
Evangelii Gaudium, 121 and 272
www.vatican.va

38: Having Faith
General Audience, October 2, 2013
www.vatican.va

39: Faith and Doubt
General Audience, November 23, 2016
www.vatican.va

40: Faith Is Fidelity
General Audience, November 23, 2016
www.vatican.va
Homily, October 13, 2013
www.vatican.va

41: Faith-Knowledge
Lumen Fidei, 28
www.vatican.val

42: Keeping the Faith
Homily, January 6, 2014
www.vatican.va

43: The Obedience of Faith
Lumen Fidei, 29
Lumen Fidei, 30
www.vatican.va

44: Right Faith
Lumen Fidei, 36
www.vatican.va

45: Faith Awakens
Lumen Fidei, 34
www.vatican.va

46: Faith and Reason
Evangelli Gaudium, 242
Evangelli Gaudium, 243
www.vatican.va

47: Faith and Sacraments
Homily, January 1, 2015
www.vatican.va
Lumen Fidei, 40
www.vatican.va

48: The Faith of the Church
Homily, January 11, 2015
www.vatican.va

49: Faith Is Light
Homily, January 8, 2017
www.vatican.va
Lumen Fidei, 41
www.vatican.va

50: The Sacraments: Gifts of Faith
Lumen Fidei, 43
Lumen Fidei, 44
www.vatican.va

51: Joyful Faith
General Audience, November 6, 2013
www.vatican.va

52: God's Faithful Love
Angelus, January 17, 2016
www.vatican.va

53: The Life of Faith
Angelus, January 14, 2018
www.vatican.va
Homily, November 29, 2017
www.vatican.va

54: Professing Our Faith
Lumen Fidei, 45
www.vatican.va
Evangelii Gaudium, 278
www.vatican.va

55: An Attitude of Faith
Angelus, August 9, 2015
www.vatican.va

56: Faith and Creation
Lumen Fidei, 55
www.vatican.va

57: Faith and Forgiveness
Lumen Fidei, 55
www.vatican.va
Laudato Si, 93
www.vatican.va

58: Consonant with Our Faith
Laudato, Si, 200
www.vatican.va

59: Faith and Responsibility
Laudato Si, 220
www.vatican.va

60: Faith in Public Life
Lumen Fidei, 55
www.vatican.va

61: Faith Illumines Life and Society
Lumen Fidei, 55
www.vatican.va
Evangelii Gaudium, 63
Evangelii Gaudium, 89
www.vatican.va

62: Faith and Suffering
Homily, November 6, 2016
www.vatican.va

63: Faith Is Hope
Lumen Fidei, 57
www.vatican.va

64: The Flame of Faith in Darkness
General Audience, June 17, 2015
www.vatican.va
General Audience, October 18, 2017
www.vatican.va

65: Humble Faith
Angelus, October 6, 2013
www.vatican.va

66: Mary's Faith
Regina Caeli, March 28, 2016
www.vatican.va

67: Mary as the Model of Our Faith
General Audience, October 23, 2013
www.vatican.va
Lumen Fidei, 58
www.vatican.va

68: Mary, Faith Demonstrated
Lumen Fidei, 58
Lumen Fidei, 59
www.vatican.va

69: Illumined by the Faith of Mary
Evangelii Gaudium, 287
www.vatican.va
General Audience, October 23, 2013
www.vatican.va

70: The Faith of Our Mother
Angelus, December 21, 2014
www.vatican.va
Angelus, August 15, 2015
www.vatican.va

71: Mary's Merciful Faith
Angelus, August 15, 2017
www.vatican.va
Angelus, January 1, 2018
www.vatican.va

72: Mary's Pilgrimage of Faith
Homily, October 13, 2013
www.vatican.va
Homily, January 1, 2014
www.vatican.va

73: Faith Unfailing
Homily, January 1, 2014
www.vatican.va

74: Family and Faith
Amoris Laetitia, 16
www.vatican.va

75: Faith Is God's Gift
Amoris Laetitia, 287
www.vatican.va

76: Education and Faith
Amoris Laetitia, 288
www.vatican.va

77: Families and Faith
Homily, October 27, 2013
www.vatican.va
Homily, January 11, 2015
www.vatican.va

78: Transmission of the Faith
Homily, June 21, 2015
www.vatican.va

79: Faith Opens a Window
Homily, September 27, 2015
www.vatican.va

80: The Dialect of Faith
Homily, January 7, 2018
www.vatican.va

81: "If you *had* faith . . ."
Homily, October 2, 2016
www.vatican.va

82: A Faith That Nourishes
General Audience, May 25, 2016
www.vatican.va

83: The Breath of Faith Is Prayer
Angelus, October 6, 2013
www.vatican.va
Angelus, October 20, 2013
www.vatican.va

84: With God Who Is Faithful
Angelus, October 20, 2013
www.vatican.va
Homily, June 29, 2015
www.vatican.va

85: A Fragile Faith
Angelus, August 10, 2014
www.vatican.va

86: Of "Little Faith"
Angelus, August 10, 2014
www.vatican.va

87: A Genuine and Steadfast Faith
Angelus, August 10, 2014
www.vatican.va

88: Upon This Faith
Angelus, August 24, 2014
www.vatican.va

89: A Sincere Faith
Angelus, August 24, 2014
www.vatican.va

90: To Strengthen Our Faith
Angelus, August 20, 2017
www.vatican.va
Homily, June 21, 2015
www.vatican.va

91: The Courage of Faith
Homily, June 21, 2015
www.vatican.va

92: Ever Faithful
Homily, June 21, 2015
www.vatican.va
Homily, June 29, 2015
www.vatican.va

93: Faith Is the Encounter with Jesus
Homily, June 25, 2016
www.vatican.va

94: Faith in a Perfect Love
Lumen Fidei, 15
www.vatican.va

95: The Dynamic of Faith
Angelus, August 9, 2015
www.vatican.va

96: The Eyes of Faith
Homily, October 25, 2015
www.vatican.va

97: Resurrection Faith
General Audience, December 4, 2013
www.vatican.va
Angelus, November 6, 2016
www.vatican.va

98: The Message of Faith
Angelus, November 6, 2016
www.vatican.va
Homily, April 29, 2017
www.vatican.va

99: Keeping the Faith
Homily, October 27, 2013
www.vatican.va

100: God Always Saves
Angelus, June 17, 2018
www.vatican.va